1804

La Coruña

Spain

Tenerife

1799

Africa

Alexander's Travels
to the Americas
1799–1804

T0036525

For Ismae and Ada, my little explorers

Copyright © 2022 by Danica Novgorodoff

All rights reserved. Published in the United States by Crown Books for Young Readers,
an imprint of Random House Children's Books, a division of Penguin Random House LLC, New York.

Crown and the colophon are registered trademarks of Penguin Random House LLC.

Visit us on the Web! rhcbooks.com

Educators and librarians, for a variety of teaching tools, visit us at RHTeachersLibrarians.com

Library of Congress Cataloging-in-Publication Data is available upon request.
ISBN 978-1-5247-7308-3 (hardcover) — ISBN 978-1-5247-7309-0 (lib. bdg.) — ISBN 978-1-5247-7310-6 (ebook)

The text of this book is set in 14-point P22 Franklin Caslon.
The illustrations in this book were created using pencil and watercolor.

MANUFACTURED IN HONG KONG
10 9 8 7 6 5 4 3 2 1
First Edition

Random House Children's Books supports the First Amendment and celebrates the right to read.

Penguin Random House LLC supports copyright. Copyright fuels creativity, encourages diverse voices, promotes free speech,
and creates a vibrant culture. Thank you for buying an authorized edition of this book and for complying with copyright laws
by not reproducing, scanning, or distributing any part in any form without permission. You are supporting
writers and allowing Penguin Random House to publish books for every reader.

ALEXANDER von HUMBOLDT

Explorer, Naturalist & Environmental Pioneer

Danica Novgorodoff

Crown Books for Young Readers

New York

All alone,
in the German countryside,
Alexander watched the clouds.

How can I describe to you the beauty of the sky...?

That hawk looks so alone up there, he thought.

But then the hawk dipped . . .

and caught a mouse

that had eaten a nut

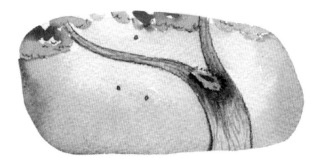

that had fallen from a tree

that was watered by rain
that had come from the ocean.

Now I see, Alexander thought, *that the hawk is not alone. She is connected to the earth and sea and sky.*

At home, his brother teased him about the plants in his pockets, his mother scolded him for the dirt on his knees, and his tutors thought him slow and strange.

Nobody understood him,
so he spent his days outside, exploring the hills and hollows.

How sad to wander about alone!

And yet there is something attractive in this solitude

when occupied with nature.

As Alexander grew, his curiosity did, too. He had so many questions.

Why do frogs have long legs but snakes have no legs at all?

Are the mountains in Europe taller than the mountains across the sea?

What is the earth made of?

Is the earth hollow inside, or is it full of iron or coal, fire or gold?

Why is there volcanic rock along the river Rhine in Germany?

Why are plants and animals alive, but rocks are not?

Why do palm trees have huge leaves and pine trees have tiny ones?

Alexander wanted to be an explorer like Captain James Cook. Cook had sailed to lands made entirely of ice, lands thick with rain forest, and lands with fire-breathing mountains.

"Where does the lava come from?" Alexander wondered, when he read about volcanoes.

Perhaps there was a small coal fire burning inside each volcano, like a flame inside a stove. Alexander wanted to see for himself.

Reading about Captain Cook's adventures,
Alexander felt a flame of his own, burning bright.

From my earliest days I felt the urge
to travel to distant lands.

To prepare for the journey he dreamed of making, he
studied everything from mold to meteors, and explored
everywhere from the depths of mines to the soaring Alps.
And finally, one day, he boarded a Spanish ship . . .

. . . and sailed across the vast Atlantic to the coast of South America.
This New World* is so different! he thought.

*See page 37.

Everything is gigantic—

mountains, rivers, and the mass of vegetation....

Alexander hiked across the rugged plains of Venezuela.

These creatures are so different! he thought.

But when he looked closely, he noticed that . . .

just like at home, the hawks were sharp-eyed, the lizards had eighteen toes, and the large cats were spotted.

Now I see, he thought, *that animals all over the world are connected.*

In a canoe, Alexander paddled hundreds of miles through the Amazon rain forest.

When it threatened to rain, the macaws started a terrible racket,
the toucan tried to fly to the shore to fish,
and the titi monkeys ran to hide under Father Zea's long sleeves.

He met many people living in villages, deep in the jungle.
The people here are so different! he thought.
But when he got to know them, Alexander realized that . . .

the indigenous people spoke interesting languages, made beautiful
music, and studied the geography of their land, like Europeans.

Now I see, he thought, *that people all over the world are connected.*

Alexander traveled west to the Andes Mountains of Colombia.
This land is so different! he thought.
But when he climbed Puracé volcano, he discovered that . . .

just like in the mountains at home, the plants got smaller
and the air got colder as he climbed up and up.
Now I see, Alexander thought, *that habitats all over the world are connected.*

Alexander traveled south to Quito,* where he climbed one volcano . . .

after another . . .

after another.

He had so many questions.

What types of rocks are the volcanoes made of?

Why are there so many active volcanoes near Quito?

How are they different from the volcanoes in Europe?

Alexander noticed that the volcanoes were arranged in a chain stretching south of Quito. He called it the Avenue of the Volcanoes.

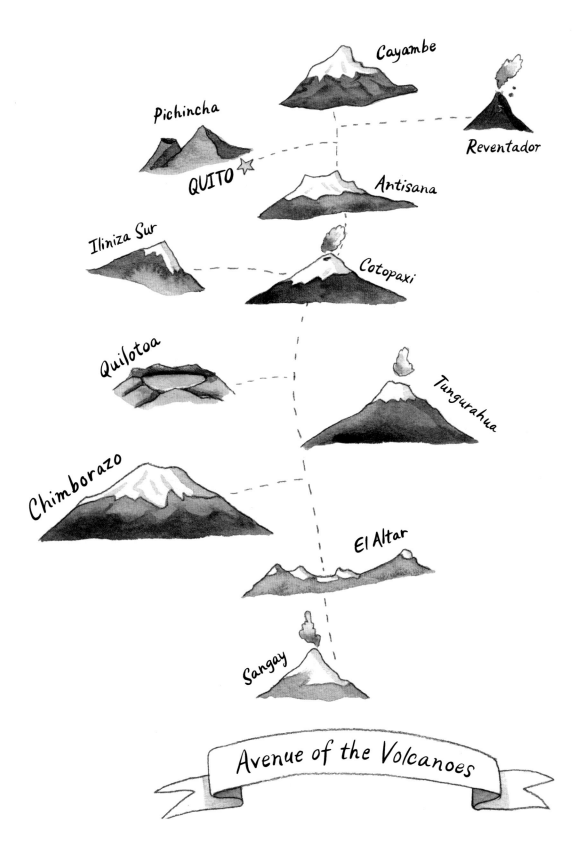

Cayambe

Pichincha

Reventador

QUITO

Antisana

Iliniza Sur

Cotopaxi

Quilotoa

Tungurahua

Chimborazo

El Altar

Sangay

Avenue of the Volcanoes

Was it just a coincidence that the volcanoes were arranged in a chain? Alexander didn't think so.

By studying the volcanoes, he understood that they were not lit by small, separate coal fires, like most scientists supposed. He believed that the volcanoes must be connected underground, heated by forces deep beneath the earth's surface— and he was right!

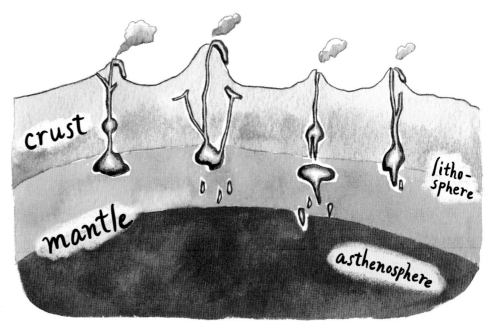

Now I see, Alexander thought, peering into the fire-spitting crater of Pichincha, *that the volcanoes must be connected to each other . . . and to the interior of the earth!*
But then . . .

A terrible, stinking, sulfurous smell wafted from Pichincha's crater! The volcano began to rumble!

We were forced to tell the people the sad news that their nearby volcano is on fire.

The people of Quito accused Alexander of angering the volcano gods by throwing gunpowder into the crater!

But Alexander explained that eruptions were caused by underground forces beyond what humans could control.

Some people didn't believe him, but many others began to listen to his ideas. Soon, people all over the world would be talking about Alexander's explorations and discoveries.

After his Pichincha expedition, Alexander set out to climb the giant volcano Chimborazo. It was believed to be the tallest mountain in the world. No one had ever reached its peak.

In 1802, Alexander climbed so high he could barely breathe. He climbed so high he felt dizzy and sick. At the snow line, his porters became frightened and turned back. But Alexander kept climbing.

He had almost reached the summit, when he came to a wide ravine filled with snow.

It was too deep to cross and too steep to climb.

Frozen, tired, and weak, Alexander had no choice but to stop.

I am like a hawk in the sky, Alexander thought, *all alone*.

But then the fog began to lift. Alexander saw the snowy summit above him and a dash of blue sky. He saw the ridges of mountains far below.

A magnificent sight.

Then the clouds parted, and from his perch at the top of the world, Alexander saw that . . .

the volcanoes formed the land
   that sprouted the plants
   that fed the people
   that were kin to the animals
   that roamed the earth and sea and sky.
   Now I see, thought Alexander,
that everything *is connected!*

On Chimborazo, Alexander had climbed
higher than any human being had ever climbed.
And from that great height . . .

he no longer felt alone.

Author's Note

I first became interested (okay, obsessed) with Alexander von Humboldt when, in my early twenties, I spent about half a year living in Ecuador near Cotopaxi volcano. After I had traveled the length of the Avenue of the Volcanoes and visited the rain forest, I discovered that, two hundred years earlier, Humboldt had explored many of these same places (though he was traveling on foot, by boat, and by mule, while I was traveling mostly by bus). He possessed a wealth of knowledge about the flora and fauna, geology, climate, culture, and languages of these equatorial lands that I had also fallen in love with. Just as young Alexander longed to be an explorer like Captain James Cook, I longed to be an explorer and writer like Alexander von Humboldt. And so I join the multitude of artists inspired by Humboldt's life and work.

After climbing Chimborazo, Alexander continued his travels south to Lima, Peru, along with Aimé Bonpland, the French botanist who had been his traveling companion throughout the voyage. From there, they sailed to Mexico, where Alexander spent nearly a year studying pre-Columbian civilizations and mapping the country, which had never been done accurately before. He was the first to develop isolines—the horizontal bands that stretch across a map to connect regions of similar climates.

In 1804, Alexander arrived in Philadelphia, along with seventy-seven boxes full of notebooks, sketches, plants, rocks, and other specimens. While he greatly admired the United States's democracy, which had been established less than thirty years before, he was deeply critical of the nation's "abominable law" permitting slavery. He believed the economy could prosper without reliance on free labor, cruelty, and oppression. "A Nation's wealth is just like an individual's," he wrote, "only the accessory to our happiness. Before being free, we must be just, and without justice there can be no lasting prosperity."

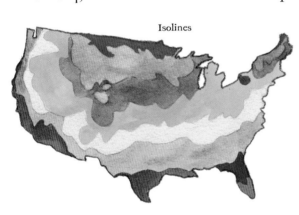

Isolines

Alexander was the only well-known nineteenth-century scientist to argue, throughout his career, that race was not a biological category. In *Cosmos*, he declared that "all are alike designed for freedom."

At the age of thirty-four, Alexander returned home to Paris and was welcomed as a hero. News of his travels and discoveries had preceded him. Across the ocean, he had carried some 60,000 plant specimens, of which nearly 2,000 species were new to European scientists—it was more than any other botanist had ever collected.

Alexander went on to publish dozens of essays, scientific papers, books, and folios of illustrations and prints, including the *Naturgemälde*. This drawing of Chimborazo showed the distribution of plant species from the base of the volcano to its snow line in order to depict the relationships between plants, geography, and climate—in other words, to describe the interconnectedness of our living world. With the *Naturgemälde* and its accompanying essay, Alexander established the foundation for modern ecology.

Despite dreams of traveling to India, the only other major expedition Alexander made in his life was to Siberia, at the age of fifty-nine. In Russia, he made some of the earliest recorded observations about the ways in which humans were negatively impacting the climate through deforestation, water use, and industrial steam and gas. A quarter of a century earlier, he had noted the drought caused by deforestation near Lake Valencia in Venezuela. Our current understanding of climate change is directly influenced by Humboldt's groundbreaking studies.

At the age of sixty-five, Alexander started his greatest work, *Cosmos*, which he hoped would unite the range of scientific disciplines—"from the nebular stars to the mosses on the granite rocks," from landscape art to outer space to poetry to biology to human language. He wanted to write a book about the whole universe. *Cosmos* consisted of five volumes; the fifth was published after his death.

In the eighteenth century, and during the time Alexander was exploring the Avenue of the Volcanoes, scientists were arguing about what the earth was made of. There were two dominant theories. The first theory, called Neptunism, held that the earth was made of rocks formed when sediments crystalized in the oceans. This theory was named after Neptune, the Roman god of the sea. Neptunists believed that volcanoes did not play a big role in the formation of the earth, and were heated by small, separate coal fires beneath each crater (see page 26).

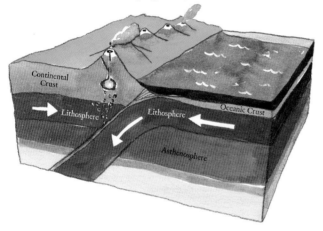

The second theory, Plutonism, held that the earth was made of rocks formed by intense heat deep below its surface. This theory was named after Pluto, the Roman god of the underworld. The Plutonists believed that the earth was hot inside—not just in small, separate fires but to its very core.

When Alexander observed that volcanoes were arranged in a chain across the landscape, he guessed that they might be connected far beneath the earth's surface by shared channels of magma. He wasn't exactly right about this—the channels of magma didn't connect to each other, but they did connect to the hot interior of the earth. Alexander's studies helped to prove the Neptunists wrong and to pave the way for the modern theory of plate tectonics, which was developed in the 1960s. Tectonic plates are giant pieces of the earth's crust and mantle that collide beneath the surface of the earth, causing dramatic changes in pressure and heat—which cause eruptions. This explains why volcanoes often form in chains along the edges of the earth's tectonic plates.

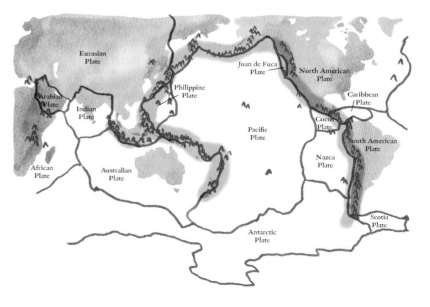

Some Notes on the Text

pp. 16–17: Why did Alexander, and other Europeans of his time, call North and South America the "New World"?

The western continents (North America and South America) were named by Europeans after Amerigo Vespucci, the Italian navigator who sailed across the Atlantic sometime in the late 1400s or early 1500s.

Vespucci supposedly realized that this western continent was not part of eastern Asia, as the Italian explorer Christopher Columbus had believed when he reached its shores a few years earlier, but a "New World," a separate continent, to which Europeans had not previously traveled. Europeans referred to Asia, Africa, and Europe as the "Old World." Of course, "New World" is a misleading name for a place where people had already been living for well over 20,000 years. Still, the name stuck for Europeans well into Alexander's time in the nineteenth century.

pp. 20–21: It's hard to know exactly what indigenous people in the Orinoco region of Venezuela wore, how they cut their hair, and what their tools looked like over two hundred years ago.

So what did these people look like, and how should I draw them?

Unfortunately, most of the surviving historical texts and images describing indigenous people around 1800 were created by Europeans, particularly the Jesuit missionaries in America, who viewed indigenous people through an imperialist, colonizing, racist lens.

Despite his Eurocentric perspective, Alexander's main interest was in learning about the culture, languages, arts, and sciences of the indigenous people he encountered, so I felt that I could take into account his impressions. Alexander described the body paint many indigenous people used to adorn themselves: "Red paint is—we could say—the only clothing the Indians use. . . . The common decoration of the Caribs, Otomacs and Yaruros is annatto, which Spaniards call *achote*." He also wrote that the Carib people were "naked, armed with bows and arrows, and covered in annatto, the dye made from Bixa orellana. The chief, the servants, the furniture, the sail and boat were all painted red. These Caribs are almost athletic in build and seemed far taller than any Indians we had seen up to now. Smooth, thick hair cut in a fringe like choir boys', eyebrows painted black . . ."

Red body paint is still used by many people in the Amazon rain forest and Orinoco Basin. For my drawings, I referenced photographs of indigenous people from more recent times, though of course peoples have migrated and traditions have changed over the past two hundred years. I also consulted with an indigenous elder who informed me that subtle differences in face-paint patterns can distinguish members of one group from another; however, it was difficult to find precise information on which geometric designs may have been painted by the specific people Alexander encountered, so I was only able to compile the clues and make my best guess. The important thing to note is that many of Alexander's travels and discoveries would not have been possible without the assistance (from paddling the boat to carrying his equipment) and local knowledge provided by the diverse indigenous people he met in South and Central America.

p. 24: Quito is now the capital of Ecuador. During Alexander's travels, he climbed a number of mountain and volcano peaks surrounding this city.

Alexander von Humboldt Timeline

1769: Alexander is born in Berlin. (The same year as Napoleon!) He has an older brother, Wilhelm.

1779: When Alexander is only nine years old, his beloved father dies.

1789: In Göttingen, Alexander attends university and meets the naturalist Georg Forster, who had sailed with Captain James Cook (Alexander's boyhood hero) as a teenager.

1790: Georg and Alexander spend the summer traveling through the Netherlands, England, and France. Georg introduces Alexander to scientists, artists, thinkers, and explorers in London. They witness the early stages of the French Revolution, hike the countryside, and discuss Georg's travels at length. Alexander dreams of traveling the world, too!

1791–1792: Alexander studies at the School of Mines in Freiberg, according to his mother's wishes. He goes on to become a mining inspector for the government. He invents a respirator and a lantern for use deep in the mines.

1796: Alexander's mother dies, leaving him an inheritance that will fund his travels.

1799: Charles IV, king of Spain, grants Alexander permission to explore the Spanish territories in America and passage on the *Pizarro*, a Spanish mail boat sailing from La Coruña, Spain. Alexander departs for America! "My head is dizzy with joy." Alexander arrives at Cumaná, Venezuela, on July 16, 1799.

1800: In February, Alexander visits Lake Valencia, where he determines the cause of drought to be deforestation. From March through June, he travels 1,400 miles down the Orinoco River and other tributaries, into the rain forest. In July, he crosses the llanos (plains) of Venezuela. In November, he sails for Cuba.

1801: Alexander begins his journey through the Andes, first visiting Colombia (where he visits Bogotá and climbs Puracé volcano) and then trekking across many grueling mountain passes to arrive in Quito, Ecuador.

1802: Alexander climbs numerous volcanoes in the Avenue of the Volcanoes, including Pichincha, Cotopaxi, Antisana, Tungurahua, and Chimborazo. In October, he arrives in Lima, Peru.

1803: Alexander travels to Mexico to study pre-Columbian civilizations.

1804: Alexander travels to Cuba again and to Philadelphia, where he meets President Thomas Jefferson. Finally, in July, he and Aimé Bonpland depart for Europe on a ship called the *Favorite*. In Paris, he meets Simón Bolívar, the South American revolutionary. Alexander lives in Paris for most of the next two decades.

1805: Alexander publishes *Essay on the Geography of Plants*.

1807: Alexander publishes *Views of Nature*.

1810–1813: Alexander publishes *Views of the Cordilleras and Monuments of the Indigenous Peoples of the Americas*.

1814–1831: Alexander publishes his *Personal Narrative of a Journey to the Equinoctial Regions of the New Continent*, a detailed narrative of his journey to the Americas, in five volumes.

1826: Alexander publishes *Political Essay on the Island of Cuba*, a critique of slavery.

1829: Alexander travels through Siberia to the border of China. This will be the only other major expedition he takes in his life.

1835: Wilhelm, Alexander's beloved brother, dies at their childhood home.

1845: Alexander publishes the first of five volumes of his masterpiece, *Cosmos*, a scientific narrative about the physical world and the interconnectedness of nature.

1859: On May 6, Alexander dies at the age of eighty-nine. He is buried at his childhood home, Tegel, near Berlin. This same year, Charles Darwin publishes *On the Origin of Species*, heavily influenced by Alexander's work. The painter Frederic Edwin Church, also inspired by Alexander's travels, exhibits his masterpiece, *The Heart of the Andes*, in New York.